I0623310

HAYDEE SPEAKS OF MONCADA

THE SPARK THAT LIT THE CUBAN REVOLUTION

1804 Books | casa de las américas

Published in July 2024 by
1804 Books, New York, NY

1804Books.com

Based on first edition published by Casa de las
Américas in 1985.

ISBN: 979-8-9910139-0-1
Library of Congress Control Number: 2024942330

Cover by Hannah Priscilla Craig

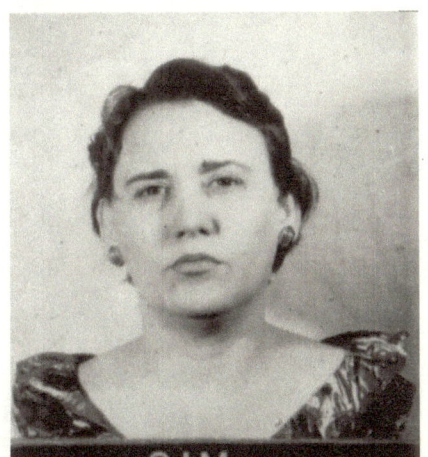

SIM
HAYDEE SANTAMARIA CUADRADO
ACTIVIDADES INSURRECCIONALES

Haydee Santamaría: Dialogues on the Cuban Revolution

JAIME GÓMEZ TRIANA AND ANA NIRIA ALBO DÍAZ

The voice of this book belongs to Haydee Santamaría, one of the most notable figures of the Cuban Revolution. A woman who became a hero. The history of the armed struggle for Cuba's true independence and social justice cannot be written without evoking her decisive participation. On July 26, 1953, she was part of the vanguard, enlightened and ready for anything, that wanted to take the Moncada Barracks. From the plan's conception, she joined with Fidel Castro, leader of the group, and Abel Santamaría, second-in-command.

That action would mark the beginning of a new stage in the revolutionary struggle. It was in the year of José Martí's centennial, when a group of young people decided to take up arms and confront the army of Fulgencio Batista, the bloodthirsty tyrant who had come to power on

March 10, 1952, following a coup d'état and with the support of the United States government.

Under the leadership of Fidel Castro, preparations for the attack began in the Havana apartment where Haydee and Abel lived. The home of the Santamaría siblings, located at 25th Street and O in the neighborhood of El Vedado, would be the main command post of the nascent revolution, a small space where dreams, ideals, debates, and strategies of struggle converged. Their apartment was searched several times by Batista's police and they always managed to evade them. Haydee's cunning and her calm way of dealing with the most complex situations allowed her to hide compromising evidence on more than one occasion.

When the day of the action finally arrived, Haydee left for Santiago de Cuba by train with a suitcase loaded with weapons. In the car, a young soldier from Batista's army sat next to her and she talked with him during the course of the trip. It was the soldier himself who helped her down with the heavy suitcase. As if nothing had happened, she told him that it was full of books. At the station, her companions were waiting for her, surprised to see her get off the train with such company. She reassured them and thanked her traveling companion, who never knew the true content of the luggage.

Haydee and her comrade-in-struggle Melba Hernández, the other woman involved in the action, did not rest on the eve of the assault. Uniforms had to be prepared and many other details had to be taken care of. By dawn, they decided that they would not stay behind and after a debate, in which the support of Dr. Mario Muñoz Monroy was crucial, they were allowed to participate in the takeover of the Saturnino Lora Hospital, led by Abel Santamaría, a key point near the barracks, and where they, together with the doctor, could help the wounded.

After the failure of the attack, the revolutionaries were persecuted, imprisoned, tortured, and many of them brutally murdered. Among the victims of the terrible repression unleashed by the Batista army were Abel Santamaría and Boris Luis Santa Coloma, Haydee's brother and fiancé. In prison, she herself would be horribly tortured. The executioners showed her Abel's bloody eye so that she would speak. Then they told her that her boyfriend's testicles had been removed: "We haven't killed him yet, you can save his life, tell us who is everyone involved in this. . . " She answered: "If he knew how to keep silent, I will not betray him now, criminals. . . !" Those were terrible days for that woman: a great pain and an immense uncertainty came over her. Only when she learned that Fidel was alive did she regain hope. If the leader lived, the Revolution could be saved.

Then the trials began and it was precisely Haydee who made the most tremendous complaint: "When they arrested us, there were twenty men with us, now they are not here, they were not in Boniato either. . . they were murdered in Moncada!" Nobody had more moral strength than her as she exposed the terrible crimes committed by the murderous soldiers. It was a lie that everyone had fallen in the confrontation. Referring to those events in his own self-defense plea, Fidel recalled Haydee's attitude, expressing that "the name of the Cuban woman was never placed in such a high place of heroism and dignity."

The attack on the Moncada Barracks would mark a before and after in the life of Haydee Santamaría, who would never manage to heal the terrible wounds of those days. Among the survivors, she and Melba would be the first to be released from prison. Once free, and even knowing that they were being watched, they would dedicate themselves to achieving amnesty for Fidel and the rest of their comrades. From the leader himself they received the mission of clandestinely printing and distributing the version of his self-defense, which from then on would be known as *History Will Absolve Me*.

It is truly difficult to make a chronology of all the actions carried out by Haydee in the years of clandestine struggle. History places her at the head of the pilgrimage to the Colón cemetery with Melba, where they commemorated the first anniversary of the attack on Moncada, or on the Isla de Pinos—today Isla de la Juventud—the day of the liberation of the Moncadistas. On the ship back to Havana, the 26th of July Revolutionary Movement would be formed, whose national leadership she would participate in.

There are many testimonies of the organizational tasks that she carried out with Frank País and Vilma Espín in Santiago de Cuba, during the preparations in support of the landing of the *Granma* yacht. Later, archival images place her in the Sierra Maestra, along with Fidel and Celia Sánchez, another among the essential women of the Revolution who would become one of her closest friends. It was precisely in the mountains, at the Altos del Naranjo meeting held in May 1958, that Haydee was appointed treasurer of the 26th of July Revolutionary Movement and Fidel's personal representative abroad. She would travel under a pseudonym to Florida where she would work tirelessly for the unity of the revolutionary forces.

Haydee Santamaría was born in the small *batey* of the Constancia sugar mill, in Encrucijada, in the center of the island, and had barely completed primary education in the rural school that brought together children of different ages in the same classroom. In school, she became Cuban and became passionate about the biography and work of José Martí. Between her and her brother Abel, they saved up to buy a copy of *La edad oro* (*The Golden Age*). In full adolescence and appreciating the differences with other families of the mill, she would become aware of the abuses perpetrated by the landowners against the most humble workers. Also decisive for her was the example of dignity embodied in the activism of the Black, communist worker leader, Jesús Menéndez, from whom they learned to know the Cuban peasantry better, and whose assassination in 1948 would shake them.

Her brother Abel had barely had barely left their hometown when he asked Haydee to go with him to Havana. She had wanted to train as a nurse but had not succeeded. In the capital, inspired by the preaching of Eduardo Chibás,* both siblings joined the Orthodox Youth. Batista's coup d'état would destroy any hope of change. Along with other comrades, they started the clandestine publication of the underground

---

*   Eduardo Chibás was a progressive and patriotic Cuban political leader who founded the Orthodox Party and took an outspoken stance against corruption and gangsterism.

newspaper *Son los mismos* or *They Are the Same*. It is then that they met Fidel and together with him they led the new stage of the struggle, which would not stop until the triumph of January 1959—a moment in which, according to Haydee, great joy and great pain converged in her. On one hand, the joy of victory, on the other, the grief for those who could not see that moment.

Haydee Santamaría's life would be marked by these mixed feelings. Only continuous and daily work in favor of the revolutionary project would alleviate the pain of her old wounds. It would not be long after the triumph when she found a task to which to devote herself with all her might. In April 1959, Haydee was entrusted with the creation of Casa de las Américas, with the purpose of working for cultural integration in Latin America and the Caribbean, following what was proposed by Bolívar and Martí. The entire work of the house stands on the solid foundations created by her and are marked by her sensitivity.

It is an admirable fact that a woman with so little education could lead a project that brought together the most valuable intelligentsia of the continent. There is no doubt that her spirit, hardened in the tremendous years of the revolutionary struggle, her ability to always stand by the most needy, and her way of thinking and creating the future, together with that sensitivity—with which, and according to her own words "you get to everything"—made her an enormously attractive figure. It is enough to read her letters which she exchanged with notable writers and artists to appreciate the very human bond that connected them, first with Haydee, then with the House and, by extension, with the Cuban Revolution.

Under Haydee's guidance, Casa de las Américas convened its Literary Prize, began to publish a collection of classics of the literature of our America, promoted a theatre festival and a musical composition contest, held the Protest Song Meeting, sent exhibitions of Cuban painters to various countries of the continent, and started a collection of folk and contemporary art. The institution, through Haydee, provided a space for recognition and dialogue for young Cuban troubadours who, victims of misunderstanding and dogmatism, found in her an open person who protected them and helped them understand what the Revolution achieved from the generation to which she belonged, and how the youngest could participate and contribute to this process.

Endorsed by a very high morale and a history of total commitment to Fidel and the Revolution, Haydee Santamaría, who had been part of the national leadership of the July 26th Revo-

lutionary Movement, would also be part of the
Central Committee of the Communist Party
of Cuba, of the Council of State, and of the
parliament to the National Assembly of People's
Power. In 1967, she was entrusted with the pres-
idency of the Latin American Solidarity Organization (OLAS). Her understanding of the ideas
of Marx and Lenin would be deeply connected
with the thought of Bolívar, Martí, and, especially, with the internationalist ideology of Che
Guevara, to whom she had very strong ties. Her
letter addressed to the fallen guerrilla in Bolivia is
undoubtedly one of the most moving documents
in the history of our peoples of the South.

Many times, Haydee traveled the world rep-
resenting the Cuban Revolution. In 1968, she
visited the Democratic Republic of Vietnam and
met Hồ Chí Minh, a leader who greatly impressed
her and for whom she felt a deep affection. Her
encounter with the land of Hồ Chí Minh was an
episode full of emotions, learnings, and reaffirma-
tions around her ways of thinking and acting. She
visited him in the middle of the War of Resistance
against the United States, as it is known in the
Asian country. Hers was a gesture of support,
an embrace in the certainty that the fight against
Yankee imperialism was a united one.

In Haydee, everything is connected to an
unbridled passion, to her infinite love for the

humblest people, to her deep sense of justice, to the commitment to the project that she started on July 26 that, as she herself said, changed everything. Today, we know that the terrible pain she suffered when she learned of the torture and murder of Abel and Boris, later increased with the fall of Che in Bolivia in 1967 and by the physical disappearance of Celia Sánchez in 1980, were still present in her daily life and ended up irreversibly disturbing her health, which led her to suicide. She died on July 28, 1980, but as the poet Cintio Vitier said, she had been "closer to death since the penultimate shot of the Moncada was fired."

After her unexpected death, she became an even greater symbol; and although many do not understand her behavior, there is no right to judge her. Her exemplary revolutionary and human trajectory continues to be a guide and an inspiration. One hundred years after the birth of its founder and guide, at Casa de las Américas we keep her legacy alive and share her ideas.

We thank The People's Forum for the possibility of making known, in English, the complete version of this text in which the testimony of her epic, her motivations, and dreams are summarized. Published under the title *Haydee habla del Moncada*, it includes the exchange she had in 1967 with students from the School of Political

Sciences of the University of Havana. This testimony constitutes an excellent introduction to the life and work of an immense woman, who still has much to tell us about the anti-imperialist struggles and the cultural identity of our peoples in resistance.

HAYDEE SPEAKS OF MONCADA

HAYDEE SANTAMARÍA

THE MONCADA:
A BEFORE AND AFTER

This book is a transcription of a talk that took place at the School of Political Sciences of the University of Havana on July 13, 1967. Originally published under the title Haydee habla del Moncada, *the version reproduced here is taken from the edition produced by the Casa de las Américas in 1985, but edited for a new audience. The footnotes are new to this edition.*

Comrades:

When we[*] were invited to come here to talk about July 26, as always, our first reaction was to refuse. We always do this, because it's been fourteen years of talking about something that, even if it's boundless, is always difficult to talk about.

In my case, I have also spoken in some interviews, albeit quite informal ones, although the journalists have formalized them with the skill they must have in that. But I have never spoken about it in public, to any audience big or small.

It happens that I'm not very good at speaking: it is not the easiest thing for me to do in my work. Perhaps it feels easier to speak when you're talking about your daily work, what you work on, what you do, what you produce, what you create. But to speak on something that, we could say, was not done to produce, to create, to do—or rather for a different kind of creation than what we do today . . . It is much easier for us to talk about our work, any work, about anything else from these last eight years.

---

[*]   It should be taken into account for the translation that Haydee almost always spoke in the first person plural (or plural of *modestia*, as it is also called in Spanish). Although she referred only to herself, it was a form widely used to a large extent of the revolutionary period, where the sense of the community was paramount.

Oftentimes we ask ourselves: Why is it so difficult for us to talk about something that was not difficult for us to do? But we cannot answer that ourselves. There are times when a thing like that is done, and we think we have, if not forgotten, tried to forget, but we realize that it is not so. So many memories and thoughts come to our mind that they come much faster than we can express them. It is difficult to be able to express what we think, because there are a thousand thoughts all at once but only one can be said.

Something happens to us with dates, because what is loved always lives on, but the dates themselves bring something to our memory, to our feelings, that makes it harder for us to speak. Because these days we remember that, fourteen years ago, a group of heroes who we knew, who we loved, fell—although they remained forever in history and in men.

Like all Cubans, those of us who went to Moncada have lived through many things: some greater, some smaller, but all with a very deep significance. We have asked ourselves, why, if we have lived after the Moncada, the Sierra Maestra—and before the Sierra, the underground—if we survived the battles of 1959, and later Girón,* historic events, why is the Moncada

---

* Playa Girón was the attempted coup and invasion of Cuba in April 1961, backed by the US government and CIA.

different from all the others? But this does not mean that we love one more than the other.

At times I've said—I don't know if it was in an interview or speaking to someone else—that the reason for this came to me very clearly when my son was born. When my son Abel was born, there were difficult moments, moments equal to those that any woman has when she is in labor, very difficult ones. There were moments of terrible pain, pain that tore my insides and, on the other hand, there was also the strength to keep from crying, or screaming, or cursing. When such pain occurs, one curses, shouts, and cries—but how do you have the strength not to cry and curse when there is pain? Because a child is coming.

In those moments, I realized what the Moncada was. Despite those pains, that feeling of being lost, that anguish, more pain than any pain, how could we not curse and how could we not cry and how could we remain as calm as we were? We think that only through knowing that the arrival of something great is coming can those pains be resisted.

The arrival of the child, the child we have been awaiting—they cannot be greeted with tears or screams. Above all, I speak of the first

---

Generally referred to in the American press as the "Bay of Pigs," the attempt was thwarted. It was the first time the US government had to pay reparations for a foreign invasion.

child. The first is not loved more than the second or more than the last. But the first one is different: we are not prepared to receive them, we do not know if we will be able to endure the pain, we do not know if we will be a good mother, we do not know if we will know how to raise them. That experience produces something different for the second and third or others who come later, because we already know that we can resist, that we do know how to raise them. We want that second or third child just like the first, but that first child is the unexpected one, it is the one we can never be fully prepared for.

And through that experience, it was very clearly revealed to me what the Moncada had been. It was not the fact that we could love one action most or best, but that it was the first: that first child that we were not sure we could face, how much we would be able to endure. And perhaps we were prepared to see some people die, to leave there those who should have lived for many more years. But the unexpected also happens: we were not prepared to experience what we experienced there.

Until then, we knew that terrible things happened: we had heard a lot about what men were capable of. But our faith in men always made us think they were men in the end; and because of our faith in men, we were incapable of thinking that a society could turn men into monsters.

Seeing it happen was a shock, a pain, a joy, that totally changed our lives; so much so, that we always talk in terms of "before" and "after." When we talk casually referring to insignificant events in our lives, we say: "This happened before . . . " or we say: "This happened after . . . " In other words, "before the Moncada" and "after the Moncada."

The transformation after Moncada was total. We were still the same people, full of passion, and capable of the same passion, but the transformation was great—so great, that if we had not planned ahead for the future, we would have had trouble continuing to live or to at least remain normal.

There, we clearly realized that the problem was not to change one man—the problem was to change the system. But it also becomes clear that if we had not gone there to change a man, perhaps the system would not have been changed.

In prison, we thought about how much we had left to do and the enormous will power it would take to do it. Because we always remember—and it is as fresh in our mind as if it were that first day—when Abel told us: "After this, it is going to be more difficult to live than to die;

therefore you have to be braver than us because we are going to die, and you, Melba and Haydee, have to live.* You have to be stronger than us. This is the harder thing to do." Those words helped us through the most terrible hours we could have lived through, and they helped us to live.

Perhaps it is a bit hard for you students to understand, since today everything is different. Today, we go off to fight with the full support of the nation, with all the support of loved ones. Back then, we were preparing for a battle without the support of the people—and if they were behind us, we had no way of knowing—and without the support of our own families. And it is difficult to prepare for a fight like that.

Today, our parents are proud to see us take up arms to go fight the enemy. But at Moncada, they thought we were crazy. In those moments, we inflicted pain on the people we loved most, and we felt grieved to cause them such pain and sorry they did not understand us. We were also sorry that we grieved them so deeply, and we were sad to think that our children might remember us as mad, as a bunch of fools.

This is not to say that we did not have faith in our people or in our children; rather, that

---

*   Melba Hernández, Haydee's comrade in struggle (and later Cuban diplomat) who fought in the Moncada, survived, and was imprisoned with Haydee.

when acts endure, they stand as the acts of a few unrelenting men. The Moncada is made great through the courage of those who died and by the strength of those who live. The Moncada would have been nothing without the bravery of those who died and without the bravery of those who lived. And we had that fear, that concern: What will they think of us, at least for these first years? That fear was deep, it was infinite, because we were going to give everything and we were going to gain everything.

We know that having gone there was not this heroic thing either, but a privilege. Many women, given the chance to be near an Abel, a Boris,** a Fidel—and so many others that naming them would be an endless list—they would have gone. But they did not have that privilege as we did.

Still, it was difficult. What girl today of eighteen, twenty, or twenty-five years old is afraid to take up arms today? The fear today is not of holding the gun; the fear is of what their son or little nephew will say if they do not take up the gun, that's the fear of today.

Before, it was a big concern for us what our little niece, who was two at the time, would say about us when she was older. That little girl meant a lot to Abel and me, and we were worried

---

** Boris Luis Santa Coloma, Haydee's fiancé.

about what she might say. But how different it is today! Today, the concern is when my son, Abel, asks my father: "And why don't *you* wear olive green?" I want to express this sentiment, so that you also understand how different the times were.

In the past, a child could say, "My father did not love me, he went away and left me without food, without a home." That was the past. But how different it is today! The child asks: "Are you a vanguard? Did you go to the fields? Did you go to Girón? Are you a militiaman, why don't you wear olive green?" Today our children push us even further, despite whatever strength that we may already possess.

Still, there was pain before Moncada, the pain of hearing José Luis Tassende[*] say: "I always loved my daughter, I did not abandon her. I came here because of how much I love her." He wasn't sure his daughter would ever know that, so he would repeat it to us again and again instead.

We heard other comrades say: "Maybe my mother thinks I don't love her because I am causing her this pain, and maybe in this moment I love her more than I have ever loved her." Even today, for mothers the pride is different, though the pain is the same.

---

[*]   Cuban revolutionary who was killed at Moncada, at twenty-eight years old.

Only now have we started to reflect on how difficult that was—and what a contradiction consid-
ering how easily we did everything then. Seldom
in our lives were we happier than when our small
group was preparing for Moncada. We didn't
know what Moncada was going to be, but it
didn't matter, because no matter what, it would
be the Moncada. Seldom were we happier than
when groups like ours, a small group . . . Perhaps
at this moment I am remembering all those
who used to visit Abel and I in the apartment
we shared on 25th Street [in Havana]. In that
apartment, it felt like there were no problems at
all; everyone went there, everything was done
there. We lived there for days, months, with no
sad moments—perhaps as we have never lived
before or since. Because afterwards the struggle
was greater, the groups were larger, and the fight
had spread across the whole island.

But in spite of being concentrated, holed up
in that tiny apartment—*because* it was a little
piece of apartment—we all made enough room,
we all ate, we all lived, and we were all happy. We
had never eaten tastier foods than the food we ate
together, we have never shared anything like we
shared that little place. We cooked for five, and
twenty would arrive. The twenty would eat—at
least they felt they were eating, because there was
very little to share from five to twenty; even for

five the food was scarce. But the joy of being there all together, the joy of sharing everything . . . In that little place, we all slept and we all had enough room. The floor felt like the bounciest, most comfortable mattress in the world!

That is why I say that it was easy, even if the thought of family, the thought of what was to come, the thought of their pain and misunderstanding—perhaps the hardest part—crossed everyone's minds. But we knew where our duties lay and that sooner or later they would understand. Or at least that is what we had to think.

It has always been hard to go back to that apartment that we remember as full of life, full of people, for no other reason than that it tortures us to think that there is no life there now. Today, it is arranged as it was in those days, but there is no life in it! Perhaps, if instead of just setting it up like that, if there was life, if there were students, if it was always full, if we could see those same men living there, it would be easier to go back. But it is hard to see that there is no life there when there once was so much. From that apartment—as many or all of you will already know because you would have read about it many times—we split into different groups and departed for Santiago.*

---

*   After gathering in Havana, the fighters drove to Siboney, a town twenty miles east of Santiago. There, they had

If we had recorded all the conversations, events, and life that happened there, it would be immense. We would be able to remember all the conversations, all the comrades full of happiness and worries. Because it was different from today, comrades, it was very different from today. But no matter how long you talk, no matter how much you want to say, you wouldn't be able to capture all that life in a hundred years.

To buy rifles, to buy bullets, we had to stop eating. Our comrades had to quit smoking; they had to stop drinking the little three-cent cups of coffee so we could buy those rifles and a few bullets. You had to go hungry just to get so little.** But the greatest thing was that we never felt hungry.

Today, we have the best rifles, the best bullets and food. No one in our country goes to battle today thinking that they are leaving their children in misery. Everyone knows they are going to fight and could die, but their children will be children of heroes, they will be children of the homeland, they will have an education, they will have a father, they will have a mother, they

---

acquired a farm that they used as a rallying point and head-quarters leading up to the attack on the Moncada Barracks. Eventually 165 fighters assembled there.

** Most of the fighters were armed only with shotguns, .22-caliber rifles, handguns, and other light sporting pieces.

will have dignity! Those who went to Moncada left their children without a father, without school, without food, without a home, and all they sought was a little dignity—something that cannot be found so easily or so quickly.

But everyone here can imagine what it was like. All those who had children thought that they were going to battle, and thought that the next day their child would not have anything to eat, would not have milk, nor a school, nor a father. Look at how different everything is today. Today they have a school, they have a father, they have a flag, they have electricity, they have Fidel!

If I am insistent on this point, it is so you understand it well; because the years create transformations in ourselves, and many times we think: "Why did we suffer so much?" And it is because today everything is different. Today, we would go to fight and I would not say what Pepe Luis said; I would know that my children would have mothers, I would know that . . . only that we all turned to dust. But if that were not the case, I would know that my children would have school, they would have teachers, they would have universities where they could study. They would have as much as Pepe Luis's daughter has today, but Pepe Luis doesn't know it.

Afterwards, events such as the landing [of the *Granma*] came, but we were more prepared for

everything then, even for our families' understanding and support. Because you cannot suffer
more than when your mother or father believes
that their child is crazy because they are looking
for life and not death. There we went in search of
life, not death!

We went to Moncada with that same passion
as when we go out to cut sugar cane, with that
same passion with which we see schools filled
with girls and boys from the countryside. Because
when we went to Moncada, we had lived all this
in our minds. We did not know if we would see
it, but we were certain that it would come. And
so we went in search of life, not death.

But even if we don't want to admit it, death
cut us off and for a few moments devoured everything. There were times there when we saw and
felt nothing but death all around us. And we
wanted to find life but we couldn't. There were
moments when we could not accept the thought
of someone living who did not have to live, and
someone who needed to live, dying. But there
were also, perhaps, the most luminous moments
that have ever been lived. Because I have never
seen such strong resistance, and with so little to
defend themselves with.

When you are fighting under a certain level of
equality, or with the full support of the people,
it is one thing; but when you are fighting, armed

with something that's practically a stick and without the support of the people—because they don't know we are fighting or why—the act of resistance is greater.

To talk of things from Moncada, many things could be narrated. That is why I tell you that it is difficult for us because we do not know what you want to hear or if perhaps you think that everything I tell is too tragic. I am not tragic, neither here nor there [at Moncada]. My temperament is quite informal. By informal, I mean that I am that way, even in meetings . . . I am famous among my comrades for my inability to lead a meeting, that type of formal, analytical meeting, because it is not in my nature. I am not sad, neither here nor there, neither before nor after. But there is a great truth: To speak of Moncada is to speak of something more than the birth of a child, because there were many things born at the same time, and there was the pain in birthing so much.

There we had moments when, not knowing about Fidel, we really wanted to disappear. We were so sure that if Fidel lived, the Moncada lived. That if Fidel lived, many Moncadas would live. That if Fidel lived, many Renatos would be found, many Gómez García, many Pepe Luis; if Fidel did not live, they existed, but who would know how to discover them as he did? And knowing that Fidel lived, we lived, the Moncada lived, the Revolution lived!

❀❀❀❀❀

STUDENT: Comrade Haydee, I have a question regarding the eve of the attack on the Moncada Barracks. We want to know what made the strongest impression on you on the night of July 25 before the attack on Moncada.

HAYDEE SANTAMARÍA: If I could put myself there, I could say more. If you want me to return to that moment and imagine myself there—I felt like a girl going to her quinceañera. That night was one of the most joyful of nights. I couldn't tell you what impressed me the most that night because everything was impressive. It moved me that I didn't know what was going to happen but I knew it would be something great. I did not know if I would see the sunshine of my homeland ever again—which alone is something worth living for—but I knew that if I did not see it again, that, too, would be great.

That night was a night of life because we wanted to see, feel, look at everything that we might never see, feel, or look at again. Everything becomes more beautiful when you think it might be the last time you have it. When we went out into the courtyard, the moon was bigger and more brilliant, the stars were bigger and brighter, the palms taller and greener. The faces of our friends were faces that we might never see again, but we knew we would have them with us forever.

And that is why the biggest impression of that night was that everything was more beautiful, everything was bigger, everything was lovelier, and everything finer. We felt ourselves to be better. We thought of our parents and we saw them as kinder, forgetting if they had ever scolded or and beaten us unfairly. I was thinking of my little niece and I found her to be the most beautiful girl on earth, because, perhaps, I thought I would never see her or hold her again. And everything was more beautiful, infinitely beautiful. The night was more beautiful—it was like something that we deserved to see for the rest of our lives, but maybe we would not see ever again.

I looked at Abel and it comforted me to think that if I never saw him again it would be because I, too, no longer lived. But I looked at him anyway. We looked at Fidel, and there was something that told us that he would live, that he might be the only one who would live, because he had to live. And we looked at him thinking that if we could not see him again, we wouldn't stop looking at him for a minute.

Comrades, maybe it would be different to go to battle today or maybe not, maybe it would be the same. But at least at that time, really, what I remember most was the beauty that was all around us, in nature, in human beings. We found everything so magnificent that in those moments before leaving, even the useless stools that we had laughed at two or three days before looked so beautiful to us!

So if you ask me what I remember most that night, it was everything: because everything was beautiful.

✳✳✳✳✳

HAYDEE SANTAMARÍA: Here, I have a piece of paper asking me to speak to Abel's political thought and plans.

Abel, sadly, died in his first act, which is to say, very early in the battle. He was not one of the comrades who died later, in the landing [of the *Granma*] or at Playa Girón, as has happened. Many of those who went to Moncada later died in the Sierra Maestra, or in Girón, and therefore the transformation in those comrades also took place in all of us.

But Abel was a very studious boy, and Abel, although he had ideas that we could call—or we called at that time—leftist, he always found an answer in Martí. He studied him for fourteen years! So he studied Martí, he read Martí, and through Martí found other things that no longer dealt only with his homeland or Latin America. He wanted to know more about other continents. So he read Lenin and Marx, or as much as could be read at that time when there was not enough money to buy books or even time to find them.

I believe—because here we have to guess a little—that in those days Abel thought that Cuba had to be transformed; but he was also convinced that Cuba could not be allowed to die. And to let Cuba die was to keep saying that the conditions for change did not exist. Because to make things happen, one has to create the conditions. Not just once, but on several occasions he told me: "We will shape the conditions, and we will continue to shape them ourselves or others will. But what we cannot keep tolerating is saying that nothing is worth the trouble in Cuba, that we must settle for trying to live as best we can, that all Cubans are miserable creatures and do not deserve any better."

He used to say, "All Cubans deserve everything, and it doesn't matter that we take risks, if it makes Cubans realize that they deserve to have us take and continue to take those risks for them." In other words, Abel believed that he had to act to show the people that there was still dignity in men, even if there was no dignity in those who had built the system . . . He wanted to awaken that in the people.

I don't know if he thought of living or dying. He always spoke as if he were going to live for many years: he always talked about what he was going to see and about what was going to happen. That is why I don't know if he said those things because he thought he was going to see them happen in his life, or because he imagined what others were going to see.

But yes, Abel had an exceptionally truthful nature, one of extraordinary kindness and tremendous principle, of infinite sensitivity. At every moment he did what had to be done. And he felt that he had to do what he did.

His political belief at that time was Cuba— *this* Cuba. I don't know what he called his convictions at the time because I never asked him; but I know it was this Cuba that he wanted. He said that everyone needed to know how to read and write, as well as how to look, as well as how to eat. And many times when we passed through Camp Columbia,* he would say: "When this is turned into a school and there are thousands of children and not thousands of soldiers, everything will turn out fine, it can't go wrong." And today that Columbia, now Ciudad Libertad, is full of thousands of children and not soldiers. That is why I think that Abel's political

---

* Campamento Columbia, located in Havana, was the former headquarters and barracks of the Batista regime's army.

belief was in this, even though I don't know what name he would have called it.

*****

STUDENT: Comrade, I would like to ask what events before Moncada confirmed your faith in Fidel. Could you name some things that made you confident in him?

HAYDEE SANTAMARÍA: Look, we—like much of the youth at that time—were in different groups. There was one called "Triple A," another group . . . I have already forgotten all the acronyms. It was a tremendous thing. I don't know who used to come, I don't know how many . . . But on March 10, we were willing to fight alongside any group, because it seemed to us that the most important thing was to reject the conditions that had been imposed upon us, and at least that rejection was a way of combatting them, even if we weren't in agreement on everything prior. But that's what we believed until we met Fidel.

When we met Fidel, everything began to become possible. We could speak about a truth and a reality. We could start from something, because before we had nothing. It seemed like everyone was boasting of what they had: as much as, or even more than ten thousand, forty, fifty thousand planes for all I know! Enough for a world war. Then we met Fidel who said, "We have nothing, there is nothing, so we have to look for it. And the problem here is no longer one of how much, but of how we get started."

We started with some old machine guns that I doubt had ever been fired. So that was already something. And then, under Fidel's leadership, we were able to gather other materials: some ammunition, some little rifles with which we could practice. But those little bullets and those little rifles didn't look so little to us—the truth is that to us, they looked like cannons!

We were already discussing plans, but the action itself wasn't specified yet because it was very confidential. Fidel taught us that this could only be carried out if it was secret. They began to look for tasks for us, to give us tasks, and we saw things unfold.

In my personal case, up until that moment, Abel was the most well-suited person I knew to lead, but Abel had great faith in Fidel. That faith became a passion in everything he did, of what Fidel could do, of everything he was going to do—and there is no doubt that this had a great influence on me as well. But then his attitude in Moncada, then his action in Moncada; then his attitude in jail, then his actions in jail . . . Do you understand?

STUDENT: So that was what determined your doubts between Abel and Fidel, right?

HAYDEE SANTAMARÍA: No, not my doubt between Abel and Fidel.

STUDENT: Not doubt precisely, but Fidel's personality became clear . . .

HAYDEE SANTAMARÍA: Yes, his personality, I'm telling you—his personality. It always bothers me when people say, "Fidel has changed a lot, look how Fidel has changed!" Look, Fidel has changed just like anyone else. Imagine, if Fidel stayed the same person as he was when we stormed the Moncada, that would be strange because even we have changed, right? Even we, who aren't Fidel. And that's just talking about my own transformation, so, naturally, it means that Fidel must have changed millions. I am an ant next to an elephant—if the ant changes, imagine how the elephant would change.

But it also bothers me when people from Fidel's generation and from the time of Moncada all say: "Well, *now* I follow Fidel, because Fidel has changed a lot." And I tell them: "*Chico*, the truth is that you were the one who changed, because three days after I met Fidel I had no doubts about him. So Fidel hasn't changed—

you have, and it is good and right that you have changed. But do not say that Fidel has changed. The one who changed was you. I was not Fidel's classmate at the University [of Havana] like you, I did not know him like you, but I'm telling you three days after Fidel came to my house, it was no longer Abel that I followed, but Fidel. And that can only be done by someone with tremendous personality and character, right? Because to me, Abel was not just anyone, but after three days . . . "

Many university students say to me, almost proudly, "I'm taking Fidel's class, you know. But look, do you see what's happened? Because look at how he's changed!" And I reply, "Don't be absurd, *chico*. Look, tell me how *you* have changed, and lucky for you that you have changed, because Fidel has not changed."

Fidel is the same, just with a whole series of other things that are transforming him. Something perfectly unchanged does not exist, right? And Fidel, just imagine what a transformation it has been. But not the kind of change where someone who knew him at the University can come to me and say, "I had no faith in him," because there, it is true that I say, "What an idiot you were, my *chiquito*, because in three days . . . !" And I'm not that smart. I'm telling you that my immediate decision to accept Fidel's leadership was not just because Abel accepted it, but because Fidel was Fidel! Fidel!

❉❉❉❉❉

STUDENT: Going back to the events of July 25 and 26—while you were in the civil hospital and after the whole Moncada attack—what was it that moved you most of everything that happened there? At the hospital?*

HAYDEE SANTAMARÍA: In the civil hospital combat?

STUDENT: Yes.

---

*   As part of the plan of attack, the rebels split into groups: the largest went to Moncada to mount the attack on the barracks, while another group went to Bayamo garrison, and like those at the Moncada, most were killed. Of the Moncada fighters, they also split up in order to target two buildings adjacent to the barracks and strengthen their attack. Abel led a group with Haydee and Melba at the rear of the barracks on the Saturnino Lora Civil Hospital; Raúl Castro, Fidel's brother, led an attack on the Audiencia Building (or the Palace of Justice); and finally, Fidel led the main charge on the barracks themselves. Haydee's unit's task was to care for the wounded with Dr. Mario Muñoz, a revolutionary physician. Three hours after the attack began, the rebel troops withdrew and enemy troops burst into the hospital having left the barracks. Dr. Muñoz was shot, unarmed and in his doctor's coat, and Haydee and Melba were the only survivors of their group.

HAYDEE SANTAMARÍA: It is difficult to say what impacted us most, but I can speak about a couple of actions because it is hard to condense something so great into a single answer.

It was a small fight, but a very significant one. It was a combat in which we had already planned, seeing that there was no way out, to die without a single bullet left in our rifles. When it became apparent that there was no way to get out and that the main battle was over—you could tell from the sound of shooting dying down—Abel, who was leading us, prompted us to think about why we should keep fighting if the main battle had ended. Then he told me: "Because the longer we fight here, the more we can save. There is always one fighter who must die without a single bullet left in his gun, if another bullet hasn't gotten him first."

I remember that impressed me tremendously at the time, because back then there was not this consciousness that we have today, comrade, there were no schools, nor universities of today. And hearing him say that, in that moment, was tremendous. Today anyone can say that, today any teacher says it, today any child says it. But not back then.

I was also impressed by how the nurses, without knowing who we were—because we did not tell them—helped us,** how they distin-

---

** When further resistance was clearly futile, the nurses

guished that we were good and not bad, how they knew that we were not soldiers of tyranny, despite the fact that we were disguised in the same uniform used by the tyrannical army.[*]

At one point I approached one of them and said, "Why are you helping us?"

"Because you are good," she said.

"And how do you know that we are good?"

"Because you are against Batista," she said.

"And how do you know that we are against Batista?"

"Because you are good."

"How do you know that we are good?"

"Because you are against Batista."

"And why do you know that we are not from Batista?"

"Because you are good." And I couldn't budge her from this point.

That act impressed me tremendously. She had told me and showed me that it was worthwhile to make all kinds of sacrifices. Because how could a person, a woman who was a student nurse, distinguish between good and bad unless she had been told? And I felt proud, I thought, "They have not mistaken us for the bad guys, although we come disguised as the bad guys."

---

dressed the rebels in gowns to disguise them as patients in an attempt to help them.

[*]   The rebels disguised themselves in Cuban army uniforms.

And so, comrade, I can talk about how it even moved me to see an enemy fall, to see an enemy die. I was tremendously upset to see the death of a person we had come to fight; so much so that it paralyzed me. Because I realized that this man had a mother, maybe he had children, a wife, and he was not born good or bad—that we had shot him because a system had made him bad, or maybe he wasn't even bad. And I was moved for a long time by that first man I saw born and die, a man we had come to fight. When I felt his body fall, it disturbed me so much that I did not forget his death for a long time.

That is why it is difficult to talk about this. You can ask me, "Why?" I do not know, I do not know. But all this does not mean that it made me weak, and that I looked away and that I could not watch them fall. Because we did not do it for pleasure; we did it because it was a necessity.

I am not only against killing for pleasure, I am also against being violent for pleasure. I believe one should have to make a great effort to be violent, to go to war. But one has to be violent and go to war if duty calls for it. But one cannot lose their sensitivity in the face of all that. You have to continue with the same human sensitivity and qualities that you had just as before you had ever killed a person. Because you have killed from necessity. It is not a pleasure to kill, it is painful to kill. But if it is necessary, it must be done.

For this reason, always, no longer in cases like this, my belief is not in violence but conscience.

When we were doing clandestine work and had to plant a bomb, sometimes it fell to me to lead the task; that is, to send men to plant the bomb. I would choose the best man, I would choose the one with the most characteristics, the most human qualities such that he would not feel pleasure in placing a bomb, such that it would not become second nature to him, such that it would hurt to plant a bomb, even if he was placing it out of necessity.

And always, whenever that task fell on me— sometimes that fell on one comrade or another— when I was in charge, I was often asked, "How is it that you send the best man for the job?" And I would say, "Because I never send someone I don't believe is good; I always send someone I think is carrying it out as a duty, not as a pleasure."

That is why I say that seeing the death of the man we went to kill was something I did not forget for a long time.

I was greatly impacted by that battle, not just from seeing our own dead, but also from seeing the dead who were not ours. So much so that we did not hesitate to heal them because I believe that the value of a combatant, their greatness, their true fighting ability, is not in firing more shots, but in firing accurately and killing when he must kill. I don't enjoy shooting, so if I can kill with one shot, I don't kill him with four.

❋❋❋❋❋

STUDENT: Comrade, I want to see if you can answer this. When you went to storm the Moncada Barracks, the comrades who did not want to fight, what did they do?

HAYDEE SANTAMARÍA: Look, all the comrades there that night were prepared to go to battle. Think of how many times had we already mobilized, believing there was going to be fighting. That is, it was not the first time that we had mobilized to fight; rather, on several occasions we had been called up as a test, believing it was for a fight. And they had all responded readily; they would always show up, determined, in the right place, asking, "Where to? When? Let's go!"

So, the eve of the Moncada, everyone went to the appointed place, just as on other occasions they had gone to other places near Havana, Pinar del Río . . . They were always made to believe that they were going to fight, to test their determination.

That night, Fidel had already informed them that this time there really would be fighting. The battle would be tremendously unequal, and so it was imperative to prepare not only to take the barracks, but for another type of victory as well—that if the objective could not be achieved, the right thing to do was to go back to Siboney quickly, pick up the reserve ammunition they'd saved for such an emergency, and that each one who still had their arms would come back, because there was no guarantee.

Failure was always a possibility due to the element of surprise, and if the action, the objective, was not achieved, then we'd have to recoup to continue fighting. If it were possible to gather weapons, we'd return with those weapons, and if not, we would return and go into the mountains with the ones that we carried and our little bit of reserve ammo. The fight would continue in the mountains, and no one could say for how long; it would be difficult. If we succeeded in taking the barracks, weapons would be handed over to the people and they would resist in Santiago as long as they could. And when we could no longer hold out in Santiago, we would go to the mountains with the weapons and ammunition we got in Moncada, along with the many people ready to follow us.

At that point, some of our comrades said they had no faith in the plan: they said it was crazy, that it could not succeed. Maybe they thought we had airplanes, maybe they chickened out, I don't know what they imagined. In any case, no one was forced to participate in the battle, so they were given a car and instructed to return to Havana, but to be the last to leave.

We believe, due to many things that are not subjective, that those comrades actually went ahead, and in doing so diverted many cars because we were just going one after another. What I mean, for example, is that one car would follow Abel and go one way, the other to the Audiencia [the Palace of Justice], and the other to the barracks— the worst that could happen in that was that someone made a mistake, and instead of going to the barracks, they went to the Saturnino Lora [Hospital] or they went to the Palace of Justice, but it wouldn't have been that serious. Or some could deviate towards the barracks—we were worried about that, because everyone wanted to go to the barracks. But the car that was going to Havana, it went ahead, it detoured when it reached the city, and so other cars were diverted, following it in a fatal mistake, not just because of the contributions those comrades could have made because they were eager to fight—the ones who were misdirected, I mean—but also because they kept circling Santiago de Cuba. Many of them were also caught and killed, because of those who had decided not to fight.[*]

It was a terrifying thing. No charges were brought against them and they were released. Perhaps their worst offense had been going ahead of the group. And those ten . . . I couldn't tell you how many, but I know it was a small group . . .

STUDENT: I think there were not that many, there were three or four.

HAYDEE SANTAMARÍA: I don't remember. It was not brought out in public, because Fidel with his generous understanding did not want to hold them up to public derision. The names were not mentioned much; no one was forced to fight.

So Fidel already had that same sensitivity and human thread in him that he has held onto since then, even in the face of the most difficult decisions. One of the things that Fidel said then was, "Don't shoot for pleasure; do not kill for fun." And the very quality that led him to say "Don't kill, don't shoot," also led him not to force those who were not ready to fight. He did not even consider them traitors, thinking only of them as not ready to go along with the plan at

---

[*] At his trial, Fidel speculated that this prevented half the force from reaching the barracks.

the time. But I don't remember how many there were, I don't know if it was written down . . . I don't remember. Also maybe some of those comrades accomplished great heroic feats later on, perhaps one of them is no longer with us because they died in Girón, or here, or there. You realize? Because one action alone does not decide your life, as long as you do not become a traitor.

❖❖❖❖❖

STUDENT: Comrade Haydee—we would like you to explain to us what you experienced after learning that the attack on Moncada had failed.

HAYDEE SANTAMARÍA: Comrade, perhaps it seems to you that this is not true, but—I tell you sincerely—it is true. I have never thought that the attack on Moncada failed!

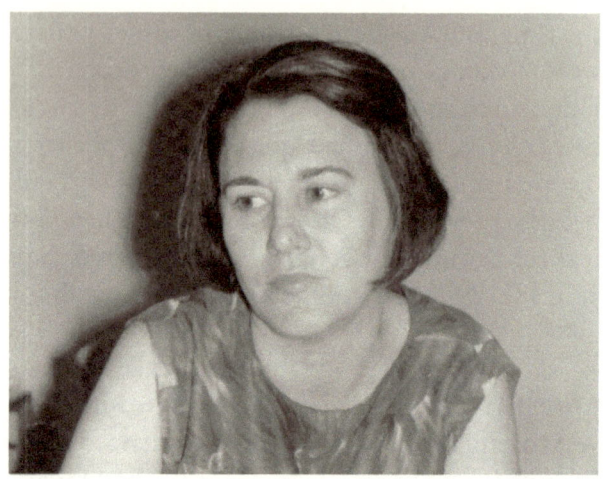

Haydee Santamaria, date unknown

Melba Hernández (left) and Haydee (right) leave prison after serving their sentence for the attack on Moncada.

Fidel (center) is released from imprisonment on Isla de Pinos on May 5, 1955, accompanied by Melba (left) and Haydeé (right).

Haydee (front) and Celia Sánchez (behind) march as part of the rebel army in the Sierra Maestra mountains. This photo was the cover of *LIFE en español* on June 17, 1957.

✽✽✽✽✽

STUDENT: Could you tell us in more detail how you learned that Fidel had survived? We have read about it, but we would like to hear it in your own words.

HAYDEE SANTAMARÍA: When Melba and I were still in the barracks themselves, we had some hope that Fidel was alive because it was believed that Abel commanded the assault. We were sure that if Fidel had died and they had found him there, they would have known immediately that Fidel was the leader.

Anyway, after two or three days—I don't remember how many days we were in the barracks, I think it was three, I don't remember well—they took us to the bivouac.* They kept Melba and I separated from the rest. We were not sure how many had been killed—or maybe we didn't want to know. And we knew that we were in detention, they took us down some stairs—I do not remember well, I do not know what it was like because I did not know the barracks—but they took us to a basement and there we saw a group of comrades. We tried to look at them all at once to find out who had

---

*   Used as a civil jail, as casual prisoners were kept there for the night.

survived and who had died. I looked for many faces: I was looking for Fidel, I was looking for Abel, I was looking for Boris. Melba also looked for many people, and among them Abel, because she loved him as much as I did. We knew Abel and Boris couldn't be there, but we looked for them anyway." We wondered if Fidel was there and we didn't see him.

So they took us to the bivouac and we stayed there for, I don't know how many days. We lost track of time, day and night, life and death, because there we neither felt nor suffered—we were beyond what it was to live or die, a fate worse than living or dying.

Then one day, we saw movement and we peeked out through the fence. The cell was high and the entrance was low, and the jail was built around a central courtyard, like the houses of Santiago. We were, I think, on the first floor; the entrance faced the door of our cell. We could see out, although in bits and pieces, not the whole picture: if we wanted to see feet, we had to crouch down; if we wanted to see heads, we had to climb up.

**   Haydee had heard her brother and fiancé being tortured and killed, so knew neither could be alive. She had also been told in her own interrogation what had been done to them.

Once, we heard something and looked out, and we saw [Jesús] Montané.* I didn't recognize him because he didn't have his glasses on—just imagine him, skinny with a beard! But Melba recognized him immediately. I didn't want to believe it and I didn't want to crush her hopes, but I looked hard and I saw how she looked and I realized that, indeed, he was groping to find his way like a man who can't see without his glasses. I thought: "That *is* Montané," and I turned to Melba and said, "That is Montané."

I don't know how many days we spent in that cell, maybe eight or nine, but no one came. We thought everyone had been captured in the mountains, because by then we were sure they had not all died at Moncada. But days and days passed and no one appeared. We knew that the supplies they had were not enough to mount a real resistance—they could have held out for a day at most. How could they resist the army with the four bullets they had left? So we were convinced they would not appear.

But when Montané arrived, we realized that there was still hope for Fidel's survival. From that moment on, we didn't move from the grate for

---

*   Jesús Montané was an accountant and friend of Abel Santamaría. He went on to become the director of tourism under the revolutionary government in 1961.

even a minute. Neither of us said a word to each other. We were so glued to the grate that, even when they brought us food, we would just push the dish back out still full. Maybe they emptied and refilled it, or maybe they gave it back to us with the same stuff on it—it did not matter. We were not aware of anything in the corridor, anything outside of waiting for Fidel.

I think it took two or three days after Montané's arrival for Fidel to appear. We waited and waited, clinging to the iron bars, until one day we heard steps, voices, everything louder, bigger, more excited than usual: we could hear many walking about, many shouting. Something big had happened. And if something big had happened, what could it be? Neither of us said it, but we both thought it: "It's Fidel!"

After a moment, I saw hands moving, some fingers—I don't know how I knew, but I knew they were Fidel's. And I don't know if I said it loudly, or softly, or if I shouted it, or if I simply thought it to myself: "Melba, it's Fidel!" I think Melba guessed my thoughts, or if I said it softly, she heard me, because she looked harder and harder, and then she grabbed me and embraced me, and said, "Yeyé,ˮ it's Fidel!" We could hardly

---

** Haydee's nickname.

believe it, but we knew it wasn't possible for so much life to have died. I don't know how Melba told me, but she showed me how to look out so that I could see his face. And it was Fidel!

We already felt at that moment, in that very minute when Fidel appeared, that we could either live or die. It was not that we felt some other thing that was neither life nor death: there, we no longer cared about living or dying. But we broke free—you have to experience it to know it yourself—of that which is neither life nor death. And already, from that very minute, it no longer mattered whether we lived or died. Moncada lived! But we both live and continue to live with the same passion that led us to the Moncada, with the same passion that all of you have for the Moncada, for the Revolution, for Fidel.

I am not going to say that we went to Moncada to make a socialist revolution. That is not true— at least, at this moment, speaking personally. We went with the idea of making a change, so that better men would rule, and so that men would not steal; but not exactly to make that change. Once I was there, I felt the change was urgent. But if we did go there without meaning to make a radical change, it was to make *a* change, and to tell our country, our people: "There are those who die for the flag," for that same flag that we have today, for that flag that we love today, although more internationalist now.

So we did not go there with that idea. We did not know much about such profound changes, but we did know that we wanted a change: we did not know what it would be like, but we knew that, with Fidel, we could define what it could be, and we carry it out as it should be, as our people wanted it to be, and that our flag would continue to be our flag.

We went to Moncada as disciples of Martí. Today we are Marxists, but we have not abandoned Martí, because there is no contradiction in following both. We went to Moncada with Martí's ideas and today we continue with the ideas of Martí, Lenin, Marx, Bolívar. We continue Bolívar's revolution, Che's revolution, with the leadership of Martí and the doctrines of Marx. We still follow Bolívar and strive for the continent he wanted to unite.

Therefore, comrades, I tell you this. Because we are Marxist-Leninists, we love our flag. We love our anthem because it is a fighting song, and it was made in battle, it was not made in peace. The song that is made in peace is not the hymn of a nation, it is not the hymn that represents a people. But our anthem was made in combat, and because it is made in combat it is combative and we don't have to change it. Our flag arose in struggle, it was painted and made in struggle; and since it was made in struggle it is our flag, because we did not make it in peace.

And when I say peace, I mean the peace that we want—I am not saying the peace that they want to impose on us. We are Marxist-Leninists, so we fight in a Communist Party, a true Communist Party, where our militants produce what the people need, where our Communist Youth study and produce what our children need. Because they have not become communists in a school and with a book, they have become communists by working, producing, creating, and studying. We are active in a Communist Party of which we are proud, to which I have always wanted to belong. And our Party is the pride of our America. But our Party is like that because its militancy produces, because it not only dedicates itself to studying in schools with food, a bed, and good water; because it studies under the sun and produces under the sun, because it is what is needed. This is how a communist is formed!

And if I tell you this, it is because the pride of being Marxist-Leninists has not taken away the pride of being Martí. It has not taken away our pride in saying that Bolívar had a reason that can be done, in thinking that it will be done, and in knowing that we do not know how long it will take, but it will be done. Because there are Bolivares also in this continent, alive, following the teachings of Bolívar!

So, the idea of making a socialist revolution was not what brought us to Moncada. Experience and need taught us that a socialist revolution was the only way to give our people true freedom.

We find the truth in the Moncada and in other Moncadas: The truth is communism!

When will we have communism? Who can tell? Because as long as there are people in need here, we cannot claim to have communism in all its abundance. As long as there is a child who dies because he has no milk, we cannot say we have communism. Now, that doesn't mean it won't be done . . . Isn't that the truth?

With deep Martí roots, today we think and believe that we are Marxists!

*****

PROFESSOR: Comrade, could you say something about the Moncada trial and what it felt like when you were in front of the court?

HAYDEE SANTAMARÍA: Our trial was long awaited . . . But there was so much concern for Fidel's life that the two things ran together.

---

*   On September 21, the rebels of the Moncada attack were tried in the Palace of Justice, but the trial was mostly

I remember that when we were taken by bus through Santiago de Cuba, at that very moment, I began to love that town as much as I loved the tiny town where I was born. Santiago had already seen that we were good, not bad. I remember how the people wanted to see the trial. And I remember when I faced that court, I saw cowardice, even in a court called "one of the best." And I stopped believing in the judges, and I stopped believing in the law, in lawyers, in magistrates. I began to believe in men. And those are unforgettable things.

I don't know if some of the judges who were there then would be revolutionaries today—and if they are revolutionaries now, they are my comrades—but that does not mean that I should not express how I felt at the time.

When I stood at trial, I hated that robe called "justice." It still exists here today and I cannot tolerate it. I believed so much in men and I believed so little in judges that I thought that justice could

---

for show. The proceedings were held as a mass trial, and included 122 accused insurrectionists and conspirators, many of whom had no knowledge of what had transpired at Moncada. Grouped among the accused were former officials of the ousted president Prío Socarrás' administration, and Fulgencio Batista seized the opportunity to accuse Socarrás as the orchestrator of the attack in a continued justification of his own coup—and so the verdict had already been determined.

not be served to me by those men with their togas and caps—I had never seen anything so ridiculous at the time. I'm saying what I felt at that time. I found it so absurd and I felt so much contempt towards it, yet I felt so strong! I was imprisoned, handcuffed, and yet I felt stronger and freer than those wearing the robe of justice who were going to pass judgement on me. And that's how it felt when they tried me.

When I stood there, I had no desire to speak. There was no need to speak to my companions, the people were not present—there was just repression and those who called themselves "justice." And for a moment, I felt the urge to say, "I have will not testify before you. Someday I will testify before men, for you give me the impression of buffoons. Justice does not wear a cap nor is it dressed in black rags—it is clothed in dignity, it is clothed in truth, and one dies to defend it."

And I knew that none of the people present were ready to die for it, or even to listen. I also thought, "Since they don't want to hear, they will." And so there I declared before them, "I left the civil hospital with twenty-five companions and now there are two of us. There are twenty-three to go. You who call yourself 'justice,' tell me where they are." They didn't answer.

At that time, although they say they weren't bad, I felt the same toward them as I did toward

[Colonel Alberto del Rio] Chaviano.* Maybe it's unfair and that's why I don't want to talk about those things, but I can't say something that isn't true. That is why I continue to detest that so-called justice and that is why I am against that justice and I continue to rise up against that justice, and I do not ask the judges anything about that justice. Because I only believe in analysis, in conscience, and not in a justice just because a book told me to. Because a human being is not like a glass that you shape this way or that way—a human being is a life. And there are not ten thousand books that can be written to tell me how to apply justice. I apply justice by arguing, speaking, but not by mechanically applying what the books tell me or what a law tells me, even if the Revolution made it. The Revolution does not make mistakes, but the man who made the law can be wrong. I totally

---

*   Colonel Alberto del Rio Chaviano was the commander
     of the Moncada Barracks. He was the officer principally
     responsible, under direct orders from Batista, for the
     post-Moncada massacre. As Fidel recounted, "Before
     dawn groups of men—already deformed by torture—were
     taken from [Moncada], their hands tied and their mouths
     taped. They were taken to Siboney, La Maya, Songo and
     other places to be killed in solitary fields. Later these deeds
     were recorded as deaths in combat with the army. This
     they did over several days, and very few prisoners of all
     those who were arrested survived. Many were forced to dig
     their own graves."

disagree with that justice, because I have faith in the human being and there must be another mechanism of justice; not in a piece of paper that says this and that. And I still stand against that.

❊❊❊❊❊

STUDENT: Could you talk to us about *History Will Absolve Me?* How you learned about it, how you eventually distributed it . . .

HAYDEE SANTAMARÍA: I think that this has already been written and talked about, but in any case . . . We were piecing together Fidel's declaration, *History Will Absolve Me*," little by little through methods and means that we found to be effective in prison—so effective that they have helped us prevent their use today [*laughter*]. When Melba and I got out of jail, we communicated with Fidel through Lidia, his sister, and through these means and ways we got it out. We went through all kinds of obstacles to manage it. Imagine! And it was distributed.

** Fidel's trial was separated from that of his comrades, held ten days after the mass trial in an anteroom while over a hundred soldiers guarded the corridors. Trained as a lawyer, Fidel took up his own defense. It took over five hours and highlighted the illegitimacy of the Batista regime—later, it was turned into a book, entitled *La historia me absolverá* (*History Will Absolve Me*), which was distributed by Haydee and became the manifesto of the Cuban Revolution.

We pieced it together little by little. Sometimes we received the wrong pages—not the following page we'd need, but the last one, other times the first—so we had to coordinate with each other to put it together.

But now that you ask, I'm remembering something that Fidel has always taught us. Fidel sent to tell us to make a hundred thousand copies of *History Will Absolve Me*. "This man has gone mad in jail," we said. "How can we get a hundred thousand copies if we can't get even five hundred?" So we wrote back: "Fidel, getting a hundred thousand out is not possible, look . . ."

"Why, you don't have money?"

"No, it is not a question of money. We have a press, we've collected money; it's just that one hundred thousand copies is a lot."

He replied, "Well, what is the difference between getting twenty-five and getting a hundred thousand?"

So I started to think it through: "Everything is set up . . . We will make as many as we can." And indeed!

So then he writes to us and says, "Look, I'm in jail and I can see more than you can. You have to get a hundred thousand. Now, it is the same amount of work to get one hundred thousand out as twenty-five. It is all in the preparation, in setting up everything that has to be done, but once everything is done, you can print twenty-five in ten minutes and one hundred thousand in twenty-four hours. Just get out as many as you can. Now, take the first five hundred off the press immediately and put them in a safe place. And so with the next five hundred, and the next, and the next."

I think we managed to get . . . I don't remember; I don't know, maybe there is a comrade around here who helped us?

COMRADE: We made ten thousand.

HAYDEE SANTAMARÍA: So we didn't get a hundred thousand, but we did print ten thousand, because when we reached ten thousand, we realized that they could discover us and we could lose our printing press, people—we could have lost many things, and that was worth more. So we told Fidel: "We got no more than ten thousand." And he replied: "That's why I told you to get a hundred thousand, to get as much as you could. Now, if I had told you to print five hundred, you would have only prepared to make five hundred and you might never have made ten thousand."

I tell you all about this so you can see how things were . . .

But that was the easy part. We pieced together *History Will Absolve Me*, it came out in paragraphs, we printed it in different ways, and we assembled it, we got some money.

I can also say that once we had it, we didn't know how to distribute it, nor did we have a car, not even pennies. And I remember some comrades, including Gustavo Ameijeiras, who told me: "Look, if you can get me forty-five pesos, they'll sell me a *cacharro*."* We got the forty-five pesos, we bought the *cacharro*. Then he said, "Look, if you can get me two pesos, we can fill it with gas." We got the two pesos, pumped it with gas, and loaded the trunk full of copies of *History Will Absolve Me*, and Gustavo drove to Oriente.

When he returned, I asked him: "How did you manage it?" He said: "Ah, it was simple; because wherever I went I would find a friend—not a revolutionary friend, just those friends that one has out there who don't know whether they are revolutionaries or not. They would ask me, 'Have you calmed down, have you stopped with all that nonsense?' Yes, *chico*, of course; I'm in business here . . . "—and then he would make up a business, I think he said life insurance—"But, look, now I have a few things to do in Santa Clara, but I don't have money and the gas tank . . . " and then they would invite him for *cafe con leche*. This is how he got to Santa Clara . . . And this is how he reached Oriente.

---

* Describing something old, like a piece of junk.

He did not go to where the revolutionaries were, because he surmised that going to where the revolutionaries were would bring about one or two things: either that they wouldn't have any money, or he would get caught with his little car, his little *cacharro*. Then he would reach those who were not there . . . At least, he did not know if they were revolutionaries, and many were not, and he would tell them a story, a story, which was already being formalized, he was no longer in those troubles of revolution, that he had formed a business, what do I know . . . Then I would say to them: "But look, look, now when I sell insurance in such-and-such place, I'll make a lot of money. Throw me $1.50 for gasoline." And they'd give him $1.50 for gasoline. And so our comrade arrived in Oriente and distributed *History Will Absolve Me*.

Looking back we can say, "How easy!" I could tell you that the forty-five pesos were difficult, that it was difficult to buy the *cacharro*, and tell you in whose name it was bought. Why in whose name? If he bought it in one of our names, he would have been caught. So who was willing to buy the *cacharro* on our behalf? The difficulties weren't just getting the forty-five pesos. But he didn't buy the *cacharro*, he rented the *cacharro*. And since he rented the *cacharro*, because he had everything in order, it was not in his name and he had no problems. That's something that seems so simple now . . .

*****

STUDENT: There is a comrade here who wants to ask you about your experience in prison, which is very interesting because you also resisted there.

HAYDEE SANTAMARÍA: We really couldn't fight much because we were alone, Melba and I.

STUDENT: No, being there, they were wondering . . .

HAYDEE SANTAMARÍA: Ah, already after Boniato . . .

STUDENT: The six-month period of your sentence.*

HAYDEE SANTAMARÍA: It was a quiet period, or at least I felt very quiet, I don't know—because Melba and I were imprisoned there, we couldn't do anything anyways. It wasn't like when we

---

* At their trial Haydee and Melba were found guilty of sedition and sentenced to six months in prison, shorter than the others since it could not be proven that they had handled any weapons. They were held after the trial with others in Puerto Boniato, but then transferred to a prison at Guanajay to serve out their sentence.

were in Santiago, when we spent two months with all the comrades. At that time there was a militant air to it because we had an objective: the trial, the preparation for the trial, the July 26 march. So in Boniato, we kept a fighting spirit, and those two months were magnificent, wonderful, tremendous, of fighting against tyranny.

But in Guanajay, for me, it was a period of lying on a bed, reading. We couldn't do anything else. Melba and I were alone: there were no more political prisoners, and we were far from our comrades so we had nothing to do. I can't remember if we ever started a scandal there just for fun, I don't know. For me that was a process of stillness, the bigger impact happened when I left.

Prison was not a painful experience for me. On one hand, in Boniato it was great because it was very militant: we were seeking justice, fighting for Fidel's life, fighting for our dead—fighting so that their struggle would not be in vain. It was not that we believed in bones and dust, but that we wanted to deal a blow to tyranny, so that our dead would not be snatched from us or disappeared, although in the end our martyrs are remembered everywhere. But in any case, we fought and fought so they wouldn't disappear. And from there we directed the job in Santa Ifigenia [cemetery] and in other places so that their corpses wouldn't vanish into thin air.

So Boniato was good, militant, whereas Guanajay was terrible—it was so quiet, there was nothing to do, there was nothing we *could* do. But the departure was also a tremendous shock. We got to turn our faces toward the sun, look upon the beautiful palms—but we were also looking at them knowing that others would not get to see them ever again. It gave us time to confront reality head on, and to despair in wondering about the direction of our lives, who would give us work, how we could sustain ourselves to keep fighting.

At that time my family already had a firm understanding of our struggle, but in any case, there was no doubt that they wanted us to come home. We always lived in the sugar *central** called Constancia, known today as Central Abel Santamaría. My mom still lives there, and my dad passed away there two years ago. Although Abel and I lived here in Havana, it didn't mean that we didn't go back home on weekends, or on Easter when there was no work, vacations, or in December. Although we lived in Havana, we

---

*   In Cuba, a *central* included the sugar mill where the cane was ground, pressed, and converted into sugar, as well as the surrounding infrastructure: the canefields, stables, machine shops, outbuildings, school, and homes of sometimes as many as a thousand employees of the mill and their families—in effect, it was a small village.

had not lost touch with the family and the town, our town.

So naturally, my family wanted me to go back home, because here in Havana, I was alone, I could be arrested again. At least with my parents and siblings, there were no misunderstandings anymore, but the problem was that Melba and I could not do anything; on the contrary, they wanted to take Melba back too. Their fight was to take both Melba and me back, because in a small town and in a *central* it is different; especially since my family had relationships there, it was a community—although not the most humble—of families that in a small town come to represent something, although in Havana or in a big city they would get overlooked. And they not only wanted to take me but to take Melba.

That was infuriating. It was maddening to think that, no longer imprisoned by tyranny, I would then feel imprisoned in a town, a small village—and I mean "town" in the sense of friends, neighbors who loved me very much. But I was born there, so they spent their lives watching over me. It was exasperating. But it was good to have the space to convince myself that I had to continue living and fighting, even without Abel and Boris, who in my case were the two people who had largely decided my life's path. Abel kept me here, eased my oppression . . . I already had to live without them, without all that they were, without what they meant for my ability to fight.

And that departure was terrible, it was terrible because in Guanajay they would not let us leave the cell except for one day of visits, where they would bring us through a courtyard where there was neither sun nor air.

Leaving prison was more terrible than the sentence itself, because when I went out into the street, I had to confront all of the wonderful things that I thought I would never see again— things that I knew so many of us would never experience again.

But we went on anyway—we returned to Havana, we lived at Melba's house. They were very difficult times. Melba couldn't work, and her father felt terribly unsafe with us there at his house—having the two of us there was worse than the plague. But in any case, we stayed there, and we continued fighting until our comrades and Fidel left Isla de Pinos.

We were living again, fighting again, we had action again, life again!

FAMILY MEMBER OF A MARTYR: But from the moment I joined you at Melba's, and with Manuel and Elena who always joined us there, I felt that our actions immediately began to take shape . . .

HAYDEE SANTAMARÍA: Naturally. This does not mean that we always kept quiet, but it was that it seemed less impactful, you know? From the moment Melba and I were released from jail, we never stopped taking action, but we didn't feel satisfied. Even with all the indiscretions we committed, it all seemed minor to us. We were not fully satisfied, we needed more action, to do more. And we both despaired at our inability to do more. Sure, we did as much as we could, and we had comrades who supported us enormously, including comrades who did not care that we were "the plague" and shared that burden with us. But even those comrades despaired. I am not saying that we did not expect Fidel's leadership. Melba and I, above all, were convinced of what was going to be done when Fidel was released. It's not that we didn't do anything— we did, but I don't know . . . maybe it seemed like we were doing a lot, but it didn't feel like that to Melba and me . . . Desperation in doing nothing. Of course, whoever saw us like this could say, "These women still . . . "

STUDENT: The problem was that your fighting spirit was not lost.

HAYDEE SANTAMARÍA: No, that was never lost— not in jail, or in Moncada, not even in the subconscious in those moments that I have talked about, when it felt worse to be alive than dead. I don't think even then that our spirit was lost.

❉❉❉❉❉

FAMILY MEMBER OF A MARTYR: Comrade, could you talk about the first anniversary of the attack on the Moncada Barracks—the first year; when Fidel went to the cemetery and was distributed *History Will Absolve Me?*

ANOTHER COMRADE: And you fought with the police and everything. Do you remember, Haydee, that they beat Lidia, Fidel's sister?

HAYDEE SANTAMARÍA: I think one of the other comrades will have to speak to this, because my memory of that is quite foggy. I remember that we went, and I remember that a comrade had to separate me and a policeman because I fought with him.

FAMILY MEMBER OF A MARTYR: Yes, yes. You fought with the policeman and told him, "Kill me, it is true that I am not afraid! Kill me, coward!" And then he had to leave.

HAYDEE SANTAMARÍA: Badly done, bad behavior on my part. Because the objective was to celebrate the anniversary and not to get killed; but hey, a year ago too . . . It was poorly done on my end, it was not helpful.

*****

AUDIENCE MEMBER: I meant to ask you a question a while ago, so you've already spoken about it a bit.

Still, I believe that I am not alone in wondering something. At the beginning, you said that right after the Moncada, you realized that changing the leadership of the country was not enough, but that we needed to transform the system. Then you explained that you went there as Martí and that you continue to be disciples of Martí, but that you are also Marxist-Leninists, like so many others who have subsequently committed ourselves to the development of the Revolution.

However, what we would like to know—since it is a personal experience—is more about the psychological shift that comes with the deepening of consciousness and with becoming a Marxist, what with all the propaganda around communists being the antichrist, unpatriotic, all those things. Was that a painful experience, of deepening your conscience until you were convinced that it was through Marxism that you could build prosperity in Cuba? In your

experience, how did that process of transformation come about? Through reading, study
circles? How did you come to your conviction of
Marxism-Leninism?

HAYDEE SANTAMARÍA: Look, comrade, in this
case I have to speak very personally.

Nothing that exists and nothing that is proposed to us in life as a necessity is painful. So,
we considered the necessities of our conditions,
and the transformation was normal, like a person
growing up, like a child who is born and doesn't
know how to walk. First they stand, then walk,
then run, then they are ten years old, then fifteen,
and then twenty. That is how it felt it was pre-
sented to me; I cannot speak for all comrades in
this case.

First, the transformation had to be total; then
it had to be ours, absolutely ours. And since
necessity itself is not painful—well, there it is.

As we continued to carry out tasks, func-
tions, we began to see the need to make a new
man, a new consciousness. We thought: "How
is that done?" Well, also by transforming the
system, and that the system becomes capable of
transforming man. There is a need for a doctrine
in order to transform man, and it was easy for
us to find it. What I did not want was a false
doctrine; I did not accept a false doctrine before

or after Moncada. Because in my personal case, comrade, being a communist is not just being a militant in a party; to me, being a communist is to have an attitude towards life.

*****

HAYDEE SANTAMARÍA: Ultimately, comrades, I'm not sure if I've spoken to you about the things that are most interesting to you, and if we've achieved what we set out to achieve. Because this is practice, we could say.

Well, I think . . . How many hours have I been here talking?

STUDENT: About three hours.

HAYDEE SANTAMARÍA: Look, it is not that I am dissatisfied with meeting with you and with our conversation, but I am not fully satisfied. Because there are things that are difficult to remember in a night or that are difficult to say, and that these are things better said alone, in a room without these "*tarecos*" [points to the microphones]. What I would've said wouldn't be the same, and I do not think it would be the same conversation that I have had with other comrades, where I start talking by accident and somehow it leads to this discussion, and we talk for hours, remembering all kinds of tremendous things. Although I feel good now, there are times when I don't see your faces—the lights are on and I can't see them—and there is no doubt that seeing your faces, knowing if you are listening, knowing if you are feeling what I'm trying to convey, knowing if you even want to keep talking about all this . . . it all happened a long time ago; and there are times when I'm speaking without really seeing you.

STUDENT: Maybe we could meet again . . .

HAYDEE SANTAMARÍA: I think it's good for these schoolmates who are studying, but not just me . . . I was a little scared going into this. They told me, "Look, these are comrades who are studying Political Science," and I was a little afraid of some of the Philosophy students. I was afraid of some of them, who were they, I can't remember now. Maybe it's something for another conversation. Maybe because of the reputation one might have, maybe even because of the amount of affection you feel towards what I might represent, or for what I might have represented in the Moncada itself, for my ties to my comrades . . . I thought, "They might expect a lot, and you know, when there is so much to talk about, things can't be told as they are." Maybe on another day I'll chat with another comrade and everything will come out much better.

I was also worried: "What are the students like there? Do they consider themselves real teachers?" So one feels a bit . . . you see? There is something limiting in it. Maybe with these same students here, if a smaller group gets together, I meet them or we meet, we could make a small group and it might turn out better. That's a flaw of mine, I can't help it. On the other hand, I think that when I start talking about something else, like when I start talking about the Party, that's a different case . . . It feels as if I take on an attitude of agitation, rallying, because it is different.

The fact is that the more the years go by, the bigger the event becomes, because the Revolution is growing and has made it bigger too—the more that the Revolution progresses, the more that people do, the bigger the Moncada will become. So it will become harder and harder to talk about Moncada.

Afterword

ROBERTO FERNÁNDEZ RETAMAR

In search of better opportunities, Abel moved to Havana, and within a short time Haydee joined him. Although Abel found a well-paying position and they lived in a comfortable apartment in a central part of the city, both were disturbed by the situation in the country. Those were years of the embezzlement of public funds, the growth of gangsterism, of division within the labor movement, of submission of the country to imperialist intrigues: former president Prío Socarrás governed the abused neocolonial Republic.

Abel and Haydee were both attracted by the implacable denunciation of the political reality made by Eduardo Chibás and by his motto "Shame on money." They soon became active members of the Orthodox Youth and met with other young workers who, like themselves, without abandoning a joyful approach to life, believed that the country required immediate and profound change. Even after the death of Chibás in 1951, they believed that this change could be brought about by an election victory of the Orthodox Party, a foregone conclusion in the elections that were to be held within several months.

The Batista coup d'etat on March 10, 1953, destroyed these hopes. Abel and Haydee were among the first to take concrete measures against the coup. Together with their comrades, they published an underground mimeographed newspaper, *Son los mismos* (*They Are the Same Ones*), and carried out an intense agitation campaign. One afternoon, Abel returned home with a new comrade—Fidel Castro.

When the time and place for the initial battle were determined and it became necessary for Fidel and Abel to select the participants, two women were among them: Haydee and the young lawyer Melba Hernández. The target: Moncada garrison.

There are numerous accounts of the battle. Throughout these accounts, the figure of Haydee is always present. Once when she was caring for casualties in the civil hospital, she saw a soldier lying on the ground. She decided to help in spite of gunfire from both sides. She approached a doctor who had remained in the hospital and tried to force him to accompany her. The doctor

refused. He didn't want to risk himself unneces-
sarily in the midst of the firing. In addition, were
they not the ones who had wounded the soldier?
Why worry about him now? Haydee heatedly
explained to the doctor that they had not come
to murder for pleasure, that there were laws of
war, that it was only humane to help the enemy.
The doctor was not to be convinced, but the
argument attracted another doctor, who immediately offered to help Haydee.

They crawled out to where the soldier was
lying. The doctor examined him. "Señorita," he
told Haydee, "this man is dead. We can return."
Haydee did not meet the doctor again until her
trial, when she had to respond to the accusation
that she had prevented a physician from caring
for a wounded soldier who was bleeding to death.
When called upon to testify, the doctor who
had gone out with Haydee under fire told the
court that the accusation was true. But the first
doctor, the one who had refused to risk himself,
energetically refuted the charge, testifying that
what had truly happened was just the opposite,
that Haydee had sought him out to attend the
soldier, and that he had refused to accompany
her because of fear.

Haydee was later asked, Which of the two
was good? The doctor who risked himself
under fire but weakened in front of the judges,

or the one who fell apart under combat but later defied reprisals?

Haydee's answer: "The one who remained with the Revolution." The confrontation between good and evil reached terrible extremes in those moments.

When Abel understood that the barracks had not been taken and that there was no longer any fighting, he ordered his men to continue shooting from the hospital for almost an hour in order to give survivors from the attack on the barracks time to escape.

This decision was fatal. Haydee would later extract a decisive lesson from the experience. At that moment, she feverishly moved from one part of the hospital to another, disguising her comrades as patients when their ammunition was exhausted. She bandaged her brother Abel's face as if he suffered from an eye illness.

But it was all in vain. Troops entered the hospital and, led by an informer, arrested the attackers one after the other. The soldiers began to beat Abel, Gomez Garcia, and Dr. Mario Muñoz, among others, as soon as they left the hospital. Muñoz was killed on the spot.

Haydee still relives those days in all their vivid detail. Fidel's words in his court address, *History Will Absolve Me*, says it all:

With a bloody human eye in his hand, a sergeant with several men appeared in the jail where the comrades Melba Hernández and Haydee Santamaría were being held; the sergeant turned to Haydee, showed her the eye and said to both of them: "This is your brother's; if you don't tell us what he wouldn't tell us, we will tear out the other." She, who loved her brother above all else, answered them with dignity: "If you tore out one of his eyes and he said nothing, much less will I." Later they returned and burned her arms with lit cigarettes, until finally, they said to the young Haydee Santamaría: "You no longer have a fiancé, because we have killed him too." And very calmly she answered them once again: "He is not dead, for to die for your country is to live."

In those moments, Haydee did not know whether Fidel himself was alive. She was alone with Melba confronting the horror, forced to discover strength within herself. She would draw out this strength as if through some extraordinary childbirth she would give birth to herself. She would no longer be the same as before, but, nevertheless, she became herself in a singular manner.

Moncada was not only a military battle; it was also a legal battle and, above all, a political battle. As a military battle—followed by an atrocious slaughter—Moncada signified a defeat for the attackers, but in the other two spheres it was a triumph. It has been rightly pointed out that the trial of the attackers was of enormous importance because it converted them into implacable and courageous prosecutors of the regime.

Haydee played a fundamental role. As a survivor of the massacre, a witness to the cruelty that had torn from her those who were most beloved to her, she gave damning testimony. Martha Rojas, who attended the trial as a journalist, has reported that when the court clerk called out, "Haydee Santamaría Cuadrado!" . . . the announcement of this name caused intense emotion in the courtroom, because she was considered by all the members of the tribunal to be the principal witness for the defense after Fidel; and for [Colonel Alberto del Rio] Chaviano she constituted a very real danger, for Haydee had been an eyewitness to the worst infamies committed by the guards on the 26th of July.

"Haydee, dressed in black, serious, very serious, without being tense," Martha wrote afterwards, "told the judges calmly and firmly the whole truth about the atrocities that followed the Moncada attack."

Haydee and Melba were sentenced to seven months in the prison of Guanajay. The prison term was hard. Even before the sentence, the two women had been placed among common criminals, who, it was hoped, would harm them. But the convicts were more considerate than the criminals who held power. After the formidable presentation of all the comrades at the trial, the insurrectionary process had taken on even larger dimensions, and Melba and Haydee had new tasks assigned to them when they would leave prison. Reading filled much of their hours in the "university of revolutionaries" which was the prison. While Fidel was doing the same in his cell on the Isla de Pinos, Haydee read and made notes on the complete works of Martí. The volumes, with marginal notes in her handwriting, are still preserved.

In 1954, Haydee and Melba were free. Their first mission was the clandestine circulation of *Mensje al Cuba que sufre* (*Message to Suffering Cuba*), a manifesto in which Fidel explains to the people how his brothers were savagely massacred. And soon the most important mission: the editing and distribution of *La historia me absolverá* (*History Will Absolve Me*), which Fidel had reconstructed and smuggled out of his prison sheet by sheet. Thousands of copies were read throughout the country and abroad.

The next year, Fidel, Raúl, Juan Almeida, Ramiro Valdés, and the other survivors were freed.

"It was like living again," Haydee said later. A dramatic photograph preserves the meeting: Haydee embraces Fidel, her head on his chest.

With Fidel free, the revolutionary process could not be stopped. It now had a name which at the same time was its watchword: *the 26th of July Revolutionary Movement.* Haydee became one of the members of the National Direction. When Fidel went to Mexico to organize the *Granma* expedition, Haydee went underground, with the name María.

Towards the end of 1956, while awaiting the arrival of the *Granma,* Haydee traveled to Santiago. On November 30, she was among the organizers of an uprising in that city that preceded the *Granma* landing by a few days. Cornered in a large house as the shooting was coming to an end, Haydee recalled the lesson of the hospital. They could not remain to be captured; they had to escape by any means. They succeeded. With her were new comrades in the movement, Frank País ("David"), Vilma Espín ("Deborah"), and a restless lawyer Haydee had met in the underground and had married several months before, Armando Hart—he was called "Jacinto."

The life of the married couple was filled with danger. Hart, who had made a spectacular escape from the Havana Court of Justice, was sought by the police just as Haydee was. In the cities, they were able to see each other for only a few days between missions. They also met in the Sierra Maestra, where Haydee found new and close comrades, among them one with whom she exchanged repartee and for whom she found medicine for his asthma: Che Guevara.

On one of the occasions when Hart was leaving the Sierra Maestra to carry out a mission, he was arrested and sent to Isla de Pinos. Shortly afterwards, Haydee was sent abroad to fulfill various tasks for the movement.

When the Revolution came to power, on January 1, 1959, Hart left prison and became Minister of Education. Haydee was named director of the cultural organization Casa de las Américas. She finally had a home. Two children were born: Abel Enrique and Celia Maria.

She also became a member of the National Direction of the United Party of the Socialist Revolution, when the revolutionary organizations joined together. And on October 3, 1975, when the Central Committee of the Communist Party of Cuba was created, her name was there. (Armando Hart became a member of the Political Bureau.)

Haydee has explained with absolute clarity the ideological evolution that brought the attackers against the Moncada to embrace the Marxist-Leninist doctrine when the revolutionary process took on a higher degree of radicalization:

> We went to Moncada as disciples of Martí. Today we are Marxists, but we have not abandoned Martí, because there is no contradiction in following both. We went to Moncada with Martí's ideas and today we continue with the ideas of Martí, Lenin, Marx, Bolívar. We continue Bolívar's revolution, Che's revolution, with the leadership of Martí and the doctrines of Marx. We still follow Bolívar and strive for the continent he wanted to unite. . . .

It is not strange that the Revolution should place important responsibilities on the passionate follower of Martí and fraternal comrade of Che—he wrote his last and unforgettable letter to her. In 1967, she presided over the conference of the Latin American Organization for Solidarity. In addition she has been uninterruptedly the head of Casa de las Américas from the time of its founding in 1959; under her direction, Casa carries out an intense task of affirmation, defense and circulation of the values of what Martí called "our America."

On this woman who was with Fidel in the darkest moments of the Revolution, a woman overflowing with inexhaustible energy and with laughter and flashing anger and a sorrow that is like a wound; on this woman who has preserved the clear eyes of girlhood, Commander-in-Chief Fidel Castro placed the first Order of Ana Betancourt on November 29, 1974. He must surely have recalled that day in Santiago, twenty years earlier, when he declared: "Never before has the name of Cuban womanhood been raised to such a high place of honor and dignity."

Biographies

JAIME GÓMEZ TRIANA is a Cuban theater critic, researcher, and vice president of Casa de las Américas, where he also directs the Program of Studies on Native Cultures.

ANA NIRIA ALBO DÍAZ is the director of the Program of Latino Studies at Casa de las Américas, which fosters critical dialogue on Latino culture in the US.

ROBERTO FERNÁNDEZ RETAMAR (1930–2019) was a Cuban poet, essayist, and literary critic, who served as director of Casa de las Américas after Haydée's tenure in the position. Prior to the Cuban Revolution, he wrote for *Alba* magazine where he interviewed literary titans such as Ernest Hemingway. Retamar went on to study in Paris and London after receiving his PhD in Philosophy at the University of Havana, eventually teaching and lecturing around the world, including as a professor at Yale University. Known for his striking and anti-imperialist essay *Caliban* (1971), Retamar became a prominent cultural spokesperson of the Revolution in the face of global repression and censorship, elected as the first secretary of the National Union of Writers and Artists of Cuba (UNEAC), and acting as a member of the Cuban Academy of Language. He received dozens of national and international prizes for his contributions to the literary world, including the National Prize of Literature in Cuba, and the UNESCO/José Martí Prize.

www.ingramcontent.com/pod-product-compliance
Lightning Source LLC
Chambersburg PA
CBHW030459130626
46549CB00007B/2788